BRAVERY

Carlotta Hacker

Fitzhenry & Whiteside

Canadian Lives

Bravery

Fitzhenry & Whiteside
195 Allstate Parkway
Markham, Ontario L3R 4T8

Printed and bound in Canada

Canadian Cataloguing in Publication Data

Hacker, Carlotta, 1931-
Bravery

(Canadian lives)
ISBN 0-88902-856-7

1. Heroes — Canada — Biography — Juvenile literature. 2. Canada — Biography — Juvenile literature. I. Title. II. Series: Canadian lives (Markham, Ont.).

FC25.H32 1988 j920'.071
C88-094297-5 F1005.H32 1988

Editors
Bruce McDougall
Dorothy Salusbury

Designer Darrell McCalla

Picture credits
Bettmann Archive, 28
Black Cultural Centre, 30, 31, 33
Calgary Herald, Glenbow Museum, 16, 17, 20, 23
Darrell McCalla, 9, 18
Government of Newfoundland and Labrador, 9, 10
John Evans, 3, 5, 6, 7
Jim Kelly, 56, 59
National Archives of Canada, 25, 32, 35, 40, 44, 46, 47, 52
National Museums of Canada, 24, 36, 48, 55
New Brunswick Museum, 26
Provincial Archives of Manitoba, 49-51
T.B. Hayward, Garland Collection, Provincial Archives of Newfoundland and Labrador, 13
Transport Canada, 18, 19
University of Victoria Special Collection, 37-39, 43
Winnipeg Tribune, 60

The author wishes to express her thanks to Mary Dohey and to Mrs. S. Holowaty, sister of Andrew Mynarski, for their kindness and co-operation in granting interviews; to José Druker and Helena Haberman for their excellent research on William Hall and Andrew Mynarski; and to Reginald H. Roy for writing the detailed biography of George R. Pearkes: *For Most Conspicuous Bravery* (1977).

Canadian Lives

Titles

Brian Orser	Swimmers
Jeanne Sauvé	Bravery
David Suzuki	Entrepreneurs
Laurie Graham	Kids' Writers
Bryan Adams	Painters
Karen Kain	Musicians
Robert Bateman	Track & Field
Wayne Gretzky	Pioneers

CHAPTER 1

Mary Dohey: Courage in the Sky

The Cross of Valour

Mary Dohey was nervous. But she sat upright in her chair, looking cool as ice in her smart Air Canada uniform. Mary never let people see when she was frightened. She had learned that as a child.

On this morning in 1976, she was not scared so much as on edge – worried that she would do or say the wrong thing. She had never met a Governor-General before. She thought she might make a mistake, especially as she was to receive her medal before any of the other award winners.

Mary Dohey was the first living person to receive Canada's highest medal for bravery – the Cross of Valour

Mary's chair had been placed in front of everyone else's in the ballroom of Government House, Ottawa, because only she had won the Cross of Valour, Canada's highest award for bravery. Mary was to be honoured as the bravest person in the entire country, and here she sat, trying not to tremble! But anyone can be nervous, just as anyone can be frightened.

Mary had been terrified five years earlier when a hijacker held a gun to her head aboard an Air Canada jet. People who show great courage are often very scared. In a way, that's what courage is. It's being scared yet still doing what needs to be done.

In fact, Mary had done far more than she had to on that terrifying flight. When offered a chance to save herself, she had refused, hoping to save her fellow crew members. That was why she was recommended for Canada's highest-ranking bravery medal.

The First Winner

Mary Dohey was the first living person to get the Cross of Valour. Although two people, Lewis Stringer and Vaino Partanen, had been awarded the medal before her, both had died as a result of their actions. So she was the first to attend the ceremony in person.

And now, the ceremony was about to

Canada has three ranks of bravery medal: the Cross of Valour, the Star of Courage, and the Medal of Bravery. These awards were introduced in 1972, and since then many very brave Canadians have received the Star of Courage and the Medal of Bravery. But only fourteen have been awarded the Cross of Valour.

The Cross of Valour

begin. The military band had started to play, and everyone stood as Governor-General Jules Léger and Madame Léger entered the ballroom. The Governor-General smiled at Mary as her citation was read out describing her long ordeal and her great courage. Then, as he pinned the medal to her chest, he congratulated her and told her she could write the letters CV after her name.

Governor-General Jules Léger congratulates Mary

From left to right: John Arpin, Governor-General Jules Léger, Mme Léger, Mary Dohey, Philip Bonné, Vernon Ehman

Twelve others received bravery medals after Mary. She knew three of them: the captain and two flight attendants, who had been with her on the plane. Captain Vernon Ehman and Assistant Purser Philip Bonné received the Medal of Bravery, and Purser John Arpin received the Star of Courage. The ceremony ended with the playing of "O Canada." Then, in the book at Government House, Mary signed her name for the first time as Mary Dohey, CV.

At the luncheon that followed, she sat next to the Governor-General in the place of honour at his right-hand side. Chatting to him easily, Mary no longer felt the least bit nervous. But she did feel a sense of awe that she, Mary Dohey from St. Bride's, Newfoundland, should be so honoured, the most important woman in Canada that day.

"Who would have believed it?" she thought. "Here I am, among all these dignitaries – " and at that moment, the words of her first foster mother suddenly echoed in her mind: "You'll be found in the gutter, where you belong!"

"Well," thought Mary, "I've sure come a long way for somebody who should be found in a gutter."

To date, the following have been awarded the Cross of Valour:

Vaino Partanen and Lewis Stringer
Mary Dohey
Kenneth Bishop
Jean Swedberg
Thomas Hynes
Gaston Langelier
Amédéo Garrammone
Lester Fudge, Harold Miller and Martin Sceviour
Anna Lang
Robert Teather
René Jalbert

Anyone can write to Government House, Ottawa, drawing attention to an act of bravery and recommending someone for a medal. Sometimes, several years pass between the act of bravery and the presentation of a medal, since it takes time to choose the most worthy from the many people recommended.

St. Bride's, Newfoundland

Growing up in Newfoundland

"You'll be found in the gutter, where you belong!" yelled Mary's foster mother. She slapped Mary hard across the face. Mary clenched her teeth, trying not to cry, but the tears came all the same.

Things had been like this ever since her mother died. Mary was three years old at the time, the youngest in a family of fourteen children. Some of her brothers and sisters were so much older that she hardly knew them. Some had married and left St. Bride's. Others worked all day. Even the teenagers went out to work. That was the way things were in Newfoundland in the 1930s. If you wanted to scrape together enough to live on, the whole family had to earn money. Mary's father took whatever jobs he could get, and he was often away from home. When his wife died, he could not look after his two youngest children, Mary and her brother Jack, so he placed them in foster homes.

Jack was one year older than Mary, and his foster home was opposite the school. This made it easy for his father to drop in and see him or take him out for the day. Mary lived three kilometres from the schoolhouse, so she saw her father less often. But at least her foster home was in St. Bride's. She had been born there on 22 September 1933, and it was the only place she knew.

St. Bride's lies about 15 kilometres north of Cape St. Mary's on the Avalon Peninsula. About 500 people live there, and it hasn't changed much since Mary was a child. Like most outports, it was very isolated — a small village perched on the rocky shore and connected to other towns only by dirt road. In winter, it was sometimes completely cut off.

One winter Mary broke her arm, and it took her father three days and nights to take her by horse to the nearest hospital, 30 kilometres away. No buses or trains came to St. Bride's, and few cars ever drove into the village. Some families owned fishing boats, but they were usually out at sea in good weather. In bad weather, everyone stayed ashore.

Children like Mary went from place to place on foot. Mary walked the three kilometres to school and back. She did the journey in bare feet, for she had no shoes. Usually, she wore only a dress. Like Mary herself, the dress was seldom washed.

At school, Mary was very shy and quiet. She felt ashamed that her dress was so dirty, her hair straight and unkempt. But she loved going to school because it gave her a chance to see her brother Jack. Even so, Mary stayed home often, because her foster mother made her scrub the

St. Bride's is an isolated village on the coast of the Avalon Peninsula in Newfoundland

floors and do other housework. Mary did not dare complain to her father in case her foster mother punished her afterwards.

Soon after Mary went to live in a foster home, her father found work at the Argentia naval base. Since this was about 30 kilometres away, he could seldom get home to St. Bride's. When he did, he sometimes gave Mary money to buy candy. Once he brought her a pair of boots. How she loved those boots! She slept with them under her pillow for the few days her father was home. But as soon as he left, her foster mother took them away and gave them to one of her own children.

Free of the Foster Home

One day when Mary was eight, she tried to run away from her foster home. Her father was visiting St. Bride's, so she went to him for protection. Mary arrived sobbing on his doorstep, pouring out her miseries. "She beats me," she cried. But Mary's father could do little to help her right then; he was due back in Argentia next day. Mary had to return to her foster home until her father could find somewhere else for her to live.

A few months later, Mary's eldest sister, Nellie, came to the school. Nellie was married and lived in St. John's, and she had come to take

Mary back with her. First they went to their dad's home, where Nellie gave Mary a thorough wash and burned her dress. Then she gave Mary a new set of clothes: blue sweater, black skirt, underwear, stockings and shoes.

Moving On

Soon after Mary returned with Nellie to St. John's, her sister went to work. So Mary moved again, to Belvedere Orphanage in St. John's. She stayed there for about a year. The nuns who ran the orphanage took good care of her, but they were strict. In any case, living in an orphanage wasn't like being in your own home.

Nellie visited Mary often, more often than Mary knew at the time. Sometimes she would watch Mary from a window, just to make sure that she seemed happy. Nellie became good friends with one of the nuns. The nun's brother and wife had had seven children, but all except one of the children had died. Looking out of the window at Mary, the nun often said to Nellie, "My brother would love to have that little girl."

The nun's brother was named Mr. Rice. He and his wife lived at Red Head Cove on the northern tip of the Avalon Peninsula. Mary moved into their home when she was ten. She

Mary lived at the Belvedere Orphanage in St. John's Newfoundland for about a year

was very happy with Mr. and Mrs. Rice. She called them "Mum" and "Dad," but she kept her own family too. When she was fifteen, she spent a year with her father at St. Bride's.

That was Mary's last year at school. At sixteen she took her first job, teaching at a small school near Corner Brook. But she didn't plan on a teaching career. She wanted to earn enough money to take a course in nursing. In 1951, when she was eighteen, she enrolled at the School of Nursing of St. John's General Hospital, and she spent the next three years training as a nurse.

After graduation, Mary specialized in psychiatry, learning to nurse people who were mentally ill. This training was a great help, years later, when she tried to talk a hijacker out of blowing up a plane.

When Mary was doing the course, she had no idea what lay ahead. But already she had a new ambition – to be an air stewardess. In the 1950s, stewardesses had to be trained nurses. They also had to be a certain height and weight, unmarried, attractive, neat and smart, capable and efficient.

Mary knew that it was very difficult to get a job as a stewardess. But she was a good nurse and she longed to travel. A popular song at the time was about seeing the pyramids along the Nile and seeing the sunrise "on a tropic isle." It sounded very different from the foggy coast of Newfoundland.

So Mary applied to Trans-Canada Airlines, as Air Canada was then called. The airline's managers interviewed her several times. Finally, she was accepted. She started work as a stewardess in 1956. Already, Mary had learned that if you tried hard enough, you could pull yourself up by your own bootstraps. "Nobody else will do it for you," she says today. "They're your bootstraps. You have to do it yourself."

1971: The Year Everything Happened

During the next fifteen years, Mary travelled around the world, seeing everything she had ever hoped to see, including the pyramids of Egypt. Then came 1971, "the year everything happened."

She began the year by taking a leave of absence and working unpaid in a hospital in Nepal, helping to train Nepalese nurses. For several months, she lived high in the Himalayan Mountains, doing much-needed work.

When Mary returned to work with Air Canada in May, she thought her adventures were over. But only six months later, she found herself in a plane over Alberta, staring into the barrel of a shotgun.

It was the afternoon of 12 November 1971. Flight 812 from Calgary to Toronto and Montreal began much like any other. Mary had often worked on the same route, and she knew the routine. After the plane took off, she began to prepare the trays and drinks that she and the other flight attendants would pass out to the passengers. First, she went to the first-class seating area of the DC-8 to ask the passengers what they wanted to drink. Then she returned to the first-class lounge, between the seating area and the cockpit.

When Mary had passed through the lounge a few minutes earlier, its five chairs, grouped around a table, had been empty. Now, when she drew aside the curtain and walked in, a deep voice shouted at her, "Sit down!"

It took Mary a few seconds to realize what was happening. She saw a man sitting at the table wearing a long trenchcoat, a black balaclava over his face, and gloves on his hands. The man was pointing a sawn-off shotgun at the purser, John Arpin.

"Sit down, Mary," Arpin said. "It's for real." Mary sat down beside him. The hijacker said nothing. He just moved the shotgun to his left and placed both barrels against Mary's forehead. "Now take my note to the captain," he said to Arpin. "And hurry back. If you're not back right away, I'll kill the stewardess."

Vernon Ehman, captain of the hijacked jet

Hijacked

In the note, the hijacker demanded $1.5 million. He told the captain, Vernon Ehman, to fly to Great Falls, Montana, and to arrange for delivery of the money when the plane arrived. As Arpin hurried into the cockpit, the masked man shouted at Mary, "Get over there and stand with your back to the window. Stare straight ahead. If you move your head, I'll blow it off!"

Mary did as she was told, fixing her gaze on the window opposite her. She reckoned that if she kept looking at the same point, she would keep her head still.

Then she heard a rustling. From the corner of her eye, she saw the man pull two wires from a carrier bag. The hijacker told her that the wires were attached to a 60-stick dynamite bomb. He called Mary back to the table and told her to hold the wires. He said that if the ends of the wires touched, the bomb would go off.

Mary held the wires in her left hand for the next four hours. She held one wire between her thumb and first finger, and she held the other between the third and little finger. She held her hand up in front of her in a half-salute. She was afraid that if she rested her hand in her lap, she might relax for a moment and let the ends of the wires touch.

Meanwhile, the nervous hijacker waved

his gun around. Mary could see his hand trembling. He had just moved the gun to the right of Mary's ear when it suddenly went off. The shot almost deafened her, and it ripped a great hole in the partition between the lounge and the cockpit. Thinking Mary had been shot, Arpin rushed out of the cockpit into the lounge.

Then the hijacker surprised Mary. Instead of shouting or waving his gun, he said, "I'm sorry. I didn't mean the gun to go off like that."

"I know, dear," Mary said. "You don't want to hurt us, do you?"

Mary had never felt so terrified in her life, but she tried to appear calm, to put the hijacker at ease. "My name's Mary," she said. "What's your name, dear?"

"Dennis," he said, giving a false name.

"May I hold your hand, Dennis?" Mary said. Without waiting for a reply, she placed her right hand in his. Then she carried on talking, calmly and reassuringly.

During the next hour, Dennis told Mary a lot about himself. He said he had led an unhappy life and had lost confidence in himself. Mary could sympathize with his troubles. But, unlike Mary, Dennis had given in to misfortune and had let it ruin his life. Now he wanted to prove himself by hijacking a plane.

More Tense Hours

In spite of Mary's efforts, Dennis still seemed excited. He would suddenly break off their conversation and start shouting, threatening to blow her head off or blow up the plane. He now held three of the cabin crew in the lounge at gunpoint: Mary, John Arpin, and the assistant purser, Philip Bonné. And he had brought out more sticks of dynamite. From time to time, he lit his cigarette lighter, waving it around so that the flame shot wickedly near the fuses. He didn't seem to care if he killed everybody on board, including himself.

The purser, John Arpin, was frantic when he realized there wasn't enough money in the suitcase

Dennis became even more jumpy when the plane approached Great Falls. He soon learned that the money he had demanded had not yet arrived. He ordered the captain to circle the airport until it came. Finally, the money arrived, and the captain landed the plane. Dennis demanded that the money be delivered to the plane on the runway in a suitcase carried by a woman. The woman was to place the suitcase on board through a window, he said. He would not let anyone get on or off the plane.

Everything was done exactly as Dennis ordered. Then the plane took off again. As it rose into the sky, Arpin counted the money. Soon he realized that instead of $1.5 million, the suitcase contained only $50 000. He felt frantic, but he pretended that nothing was wrong. In the meantime, Dennis had grown more excited and didn't notice Arpin's bluff.

If Dennis carried on as he was doing, Mary thought, nobody would survive the night. Then she remembered that he seemed fond of children. He had told her he had seen his own infant son only once before the child's mother had put the baby up for adoption. Mary didn't know if there were any children on the flight, but she said, "Dennis, I think I hear the children crying. Poor little things, they'll be so tired and hungry."

Mary's hunch worked. Dennis ordered the captain to fly back to Great Falls to let all the passengers off. As the passengers disembarked, Dennis gave Arpin his baggage tag and told him to collect his suitcase. "And if you're not back in ten minutes, I'll blow Mary's head off," he said.

Security measures at Canadian airports have tightened since Mary's flight was hijacked in 1971. Each airline passenger is required to pass through a 'walk-through' metal detector

Seconds from Death

For the next ten minutes, Dennis stood behind Mary with both barrels of the gun pressed into the back of her neck. With each minute that passed, he became more suspicious and agitated. Finally, he said: "The ten minutes are up. I'm afraid I'll have to kill you, Mary."

Mary had been praying, and she had

If the buzzer in the 'walk-through' goes off, the passenger is then inspected with a hand-held metal detector, or 'wand'. Sometimes, passengers are inspected with the wand even though the buzzer has not sounded

prepared herself to die. But she thought she might still have a chance if she could face Dennis and let him look at her. So she said, "May I turn and look at you, dear?"

"Yes," he said. Mary turned and looked straight into the barrels of the gun, which Dennis held right in front of her eyes.

"You don't want to kill me, do you?" said Mary.

"No."

"Well then, please wait a little longer. Johnny will be back soon with your suitcase." A few moments later, Arpin rushed into the lounge with a blue suitcase. Mary had never felt as close to death as she had in the past few minutes.

After Dennis had taken his suitcase and examined it, he whispered to Mary, "Do you want to get off? You can leave if you want to."

A Difficult Choice

Mary knew she could walk out of the plane to safety. But she also knew that she had more influence over Dennis than anyone else on the plane. She thought she might have a chance of persuading him not to blow up the plane, killing the crew still aboard. So, despite the terror of the last few hours, she said, "You don't want me to leave, do you, dear?"

"No," said Dennis, "I want you to stay."

"All right, dear," said Mary. "I'll stay, then."

With only a few of the crew left on board, the plane took off again. Now Dennis's behaviour became even more erratic. He made Mary and the two other flight attendants move around the plane. He told them to hold one stick of dynamite, then another. He ordered the captain into the rear section of the plane. He said he wanted to jump by parachute from the rear door. He even had a parachute with him. Captain Ehman said it was impossible. If they opened the rear door, he said, the plane would crash.

Dennis insisted that he must jump by parachute, so the co-pilot brought the plane down to an altitude of 1000 metres. At this height, the captain said, it would be safe for Dennis to parachute from an emergency window. But Dennis couldn't open the window with one hand. For a second he put down his gun. This was the chance that the captain needed. Quickly, he jumped on the hijacker and hurled the gun down the aisle.

After eight long hours, the nightmare was over. When the plane landed in Calgary half an hour later, the crew had subdued Dennis and bound him securely.

The Air Canada jet landed safely in Calgary after an eight-hour ordeal

Mary Dohey being presented to Queen Elizabeth II by Prime Minister Pierre Trudeau in Ottawa, 1977

In the weeks that followed, Mary was surprised to find that she had become a heroine. She was interviewed by television reporters and was written about in newspapers and magazines. Never in her life had she received so much attention. Yet she didn't feel worthy of the praise. Deeply religious, she felt that God had saved them all. Mary had prayed for help during her ordeal, just as she had prayed as a child.

Now that all the excitement is over, Mary carries on calmly with her life, almost as if nothing had happened. She still works as a stewardess with Air Canada, and she still keeps up with her nursing. But from time to time she gets a call from the Prime Minister's Office in Ottawa inviting her to a banquet or reception to meet important visitors. And on formal correspondence, she now writes "CV" after her name.

CHAPTER 2

William Hall, VC: Courage in India

The Victoria Cross

1827: Nova Scotia Childhood

Before Canada presented its own bravery medals, Canadians received British medals. The highest honour in the British Empire was the Victoria Cross, which Queen Victoria introduced in 1856 for outstanding bravery in battle.

Over the years, more than ninety Canadians have won the VC. One of the earliest was William Hall, who was the first Canadian sailor and the first Nova Scotian to receive the medal.

William Hall was the first Nova Scotian to win the Victoria Cross

There were two unusual things about William Hall. First, he was a sailor who won his medal on land. Second, he was black. There were only a few thousand black Canadians when William was young, and most of them had arrived recently from the United States.

William's parents had been slaves in the United States and had escaped to a British ship during the War of 1812. At the time, the British were offering land in Nova Scotia to all who joined the British side in the war. But the plots proved far too small to support a family. Nor was it easy for the black refugees to find work. William's family was extremely poor.

William was born on 28 April 1827 at the village of Horton Bluff, about 70 kilometres north of Halifax. There, near the mouth of the Avon River, he passed his childhood.

Although his parents raised him with love and affection, they had little to spend on food and clothing. William likely went hungry on several occasions. He would also have found that life can be very unfair. Although the British government had banned slavery throughout the Empire a few years after William was born, other Maritimers regarded blacks as inferior. Often black people had to put up with insults, and they had to be at least twice as good at something if they hoped to succeed. Even then, many jobs were simply not open to them.

The Lure of the Sea

If William dreamed of a life of comfort or adventure, he knew that both were unlikely if he stayed in Nova Scotia. But the sea on his doorstep offered an escape. This was the great shipbuilding period, the Golden Age of Sail, when wooden ships from the Maritimes travelled the world. While William was still a teenager he went to nearby Hantsport and joined the crew of a trading ship.

The *Boadicea*, built in 1847, was typical of the wooden ships built in the Maritimes during the golden age of sail

The next few years were filled with excitement. The small sailing ships of the time were very different from the comfortable ocean liners of today. In sunny weather, with a brisk wind behind them, they skimmed smoothly across the water. In stormy weather, huge waves crashed onto their decks. Winds tore at the sails and broke the masts. Each year, ships just disappeared below the waves without a trace.

By the time William was in his mid-twenties, he had ridden out many storms at sea. He was an experienced sailor who had crewed on a number of ships and travelled the world. But it was an insecure life, and he was never sure at the end of a voyage when he would work again. So while he was in Liverpool, England, in 1852, he signed on with the Royal Navy.

The Royal Navy defended the British Empire. (There was no separate Canadian navy until 1910.) It offered William a different life from that on a cargo ship. He was now a member of the armed forces: Able Seaman Hall. Besides braving the dangers of the sea, he would have to do battle, and since the British Empire spread across the world, the battles were likely to be far from home.

First Action

William first saw action during the Crimean War and quickly gained a reputation for sticking at his post, whatever the danger. "He was steady as a rock under fire," an officer later said of him. Hall inspired others with courage too, because he remained so calm himself. Quietly, and without fuss, he did whatever had to be done, so that his friends and companions came to depend on him for support and guidance.

In the Crimean War, Hall won two service medals. Then he went to India. India was not yet part of the British Empire, but little by little the British-run East India Company had been taking it over. In 1857, an uprising against the British in northern India reached a climax with the siege of the town of Lucknow. About eight hundred English women and children, along with 1600 soldiers, some British, some Indian, had barricaded themselves inside the British Residence there. Surrounding them, thousands of Sepoys – well-trained Indian soldiers – attacked day and night. It seemed impossible that the British garrison could hold out for long.

At the time, Hall was in Hong Kong aboard the HMS *Shannon*. His ship and two others were ordered immediately to Calcutta, from where a group of sailors and marines were to march inland to Lucknow. About four

Sailors from the *Shannon* fired their ship's guns at the walls of the mosque at Lucknow. When the walls began to crumble, the Scottish Highlanders were able to get through to rescue the British in the Residence

hundred men from the *Shannon* made the journey, including Hall.

Into India

They started out in August, in the full heat of summer, taking their ship's heavy guns with them. They faced a daunting journey. Lucknow was more than a thousand kilometres to the northwest, and they had to get there on foot or by river.

At first, the men travelled up the Ganges River, taking the big guns on barges. But when they left the river they had to march across country, with teams of oxen hauling the guns.

Meanwhile, a fiery sun burned down on them, sapping their strength. To make things worse, they were under constant attack from Sepoys. Each day, some of William's shipmates died of wounds.

The march to Lucknow took about three months. In November, Hall and his weary companions at last reached the town. Along the way, their column joined a large force of soldiers from Scotland called Highlanders. But they were still heavily outnumbered by the thousands of Sepoys in the area.

To reach the British garrison, the relief force had to pass a well-guarded mosque, which was protected by walls more than six metres high. For three hours, they fired their big guns at the walls, with no effect. Meanwhile, the Sepoys fired back, killing the gun crews one by one.

At first, Hall was on the fringes of the battle. But soon he said to his friend, "I think I'll go forward and see what's going on."

"You'd better not," his friend said. "You'll get yourself killed." But Hall went forward and joined a gun whose crew was one man short.

This gun was one of two that were hauled forward within about 20 metres of the wall. It stood right in the open, an easy target for the Sepoys above, and the crew kept moving it even nearer, as Hall later explained.

"After firing each round, we ran our gun forward," he said. "We kept moving forward until my gun's crew were in danger of being hit by splinters of brick and stone from the walls we were bombarding."

Still the walls stood firm, and the action grew too hot for comfort. Before long, the other forward gun stopped firing. Those of its crew who had not been hit had retreated and taken cover. Only Hall and a wounded officer remained on the second gun.

William Hall, VC (AD, 1857)

The following poem was written by Dr. Watson Kirkconnell, former president of Acadia University, and included in a Christmas card sent by Dr. and Mrs. Kirkconnell.

Here at the Hantsport crossroads,
Where the transports pause and pass,
Rises a cairn of boulders
And a plaque of enduring brass.

It tells of an old Hants hero,
Born on the Cheverie Shore,
In the days of the Fourth of the Georges
In a home with a poor dirt floor.

This son of a black slave father
Spent his boyhood at Horton Bluff,
But soon took to sea as a sailor
And a life that was hard enough.

He served on the warship Rodney
Through the long Crimean war;
Then shipped to the East with the Shannon,
For that was what life was for.

He offered for special danger
With a naval brigade of guns
To seek the relief of Lucknow
Where the Gumti River runs.

There by the winding Gumti,
On the level plains of Oudh,
Brave Havelock was beleaguered
By foes in a mighty crowd.

A scant two thousand British
Endured in the heat and drought,
And sixty thousand rebels
Encompassed them round about.

At last, in a fierce November,
Sir Colin Campbell came
To break their circumvallation
With an onset of sword and flame.

Four thousand five hundred soldiers
Were all of the force he brought,
But the navy's volunteer gunners
With the strength of a giant fought.

"Who will be first for the gun-crew
To blast through the rebels' wall?
For the fire of the foe is bitter,
And many are sure to fall."

"I shall be first," said the Negro,
The man from the Cheverie Shore,
And his cannon through the gateway
A mighty opening tore.

Through it, the column entered;
Through it, the whole force heaved;
Through it, they joined the defenders —
And Lucknow had been relieved.

And now in a Baptist churchyard,
Set by the Queen's highway,
A quiet Canadian village
Still honours his deed today.

The first of all Nova Scotians,
The first of his dark-skinned race,
He won the Award of Valour,
The Cross of Victoria's grace.

And as long as the hearts of heroes
In our land shall remembered be,
Men shall speak of the deathless daring
Of William Hall, V. C.

Remembering William Hall

Remembering the Nova Scotian who won the Victoria Cross in India
by Barkat Masih Khokar
Liet-Col (Ret'd) Indian Army

Monday, November 16, 1857, was the proudest day in the life of William Hall, a black Nova Scotian who won the most coveted decoration of the Victoria Cross, in the siege of Lucknow, 30 miles northeast of Delhi.

Exposure, fatigue, bombs, and bullets brought music to the ears of Able Seaman William Hall, who had served throughout the Crimean War and was awarded the famous Crimea Medal.

Nova Scotian Won V.C. In India in 1857

When did William Hall of Nova Scotia win the Victoria Cross and in what action? – S.G.G.

On November 16, 1857, the heroic action of William Hall, "Captain of the Foretop" of Her Majesty's ship Shannon, won him the Victoria Cross and was largely responsible for the relief of Lucknow. He was born in Horton Bluff, N.S., on April 28, 1827, the son of one of a group of slaves who had been rescued from slavery by a British frigate during the War of 1812. He attended school at Horton Bluff but joined the navy at an early age. He returned to Nova Scotia with rank of petty officer in July of 1876 and died in Hantsport, N.S., in 1904. In Halifax, a branch of the Canadian Legion was named in his honor.

* * *

The Work of Six Men

Hall kept loading and firing the gun, doing the work of a six-man crew. Sponge, load, fire! Sponge, load, fire! He seemed unaware that he was now the main target of the musket fire. On the march from Calcutta, he had seen the blood of women and children who had been killed and he was determined that the same fate would not befall those in Lucknow if he could prevent it. Sponge, load, fire!

At last, as yet another shell thudded into the wall, the masonry began to crumble, just enough to let a man through. Into the breach charged the Highlanders who had been circling nearby, waiting for just such an opening. Lucknow was saved!

For his act of courage, of such importance to the success of the battle, Hall's superiors recommended him for the Victoria Cross. He received the medal two years later on board ship. Since he was not an officer, he was awarded a £10-a-year pension as well as the medal. This was quite a large sum in those days, but not nearly enough to live on, so Hall remained in the navy. Over the years, he served on several different ships and was gradually promoted. He retired in 1876, with the rank of petty officer, first-class.

Return to Nova Scotia

Hall retired to Avonport, Nova Scotia, where he lived on a farm with two of his sisters. He had his navy pension as well as his VC pension, but he was not by any means rich. Nor was he famous. This was partly because he was black and was therefore paid little attention by other Canadians. But Hall himself was extremely modest. For instance, when a reporter sought him out to ask about the medal, Hall replied, "Oh, I've almost forgotten about it. All I did was my duty."

Nevertheless, he treasured the cross itself and kept it in a box on the mantlepiece. But it had no ribbon. A souvenir hunter had borrowed the medal's ribbon and never returned it. The ribbon was particularly rare because it was blue, for sailors only. Army winners received medals with a red ribbon. (Today, all VC ribbons are red.)

Hall hung his medal from a watch chain when, in 1901, the Duke of York, the future King George V, visited Halifax and the city's war heroes paraded before him. Seeing the Victoria Cross on William's chest, the future king stopped to talk to him. When a local newspaper described this, it was the first that most Nova Scotians had ever heard of William Hall. Even then, his fame was brief. He spent his last years quietly working his farm at Avonport. It was a

William Hall spent his last years on his farm in Avonport, Nova Scotia

A RIGHT RO

HALIFAX en fete for the Visit of Their Royal Highnesses the Duke and Duchess of Cornwall and York.---Presentation of Addresses.–Memorable Scenes on the Streets.–Enthusiastic Loyalty.---Decorations and Illuminations.

This newspaper account of the Duke of York speaking to William Hall was the first most Nova Scotians knew of their first Victoria Cross winner

William Hall lived to the age of seventy-seven

WELCOME

CORNER STONE of the Monument in Honor of Nova Scotia's Sons Who Died in South Africa Laid; First Memorial Erected in the Empire.—Grand Review of Troops.—Six Thousand Children Sing Welcome to the King's Son.

THE DUKE'S REPLY

well-stocked farm of cattle and chickens, with a small orchard. William Hall died there on 25 August 1904. At that time, he was the only Nova Scotian and the third Canadian to have won the Victoria Cross.

Although Hall received little attention during his lifetime, he has received many honours since his death. When his grave near Avonport fell into disrepair, the Royal Canadian Legion moved his body to Hantsport Baptist Church and erected a monument with the Victoria Cross carved on it. A branch of the Legion and a Montreal students' program have been named after him. So has a gymnasium in Cornwallis. His medals are on display at the Nova Scotia Museum in Halifax.

William Hall was the third Canadian to be awarded the Victoria Cross. The first was Lieutenant Alexander Dunn from Upper Canada, who won his medal during the Charge of the Light Brigade in the Crimean War. The second was an army surgeon, Herbert Reade, who was also from Upper Canada. He won his VC in India just two months before William Hall won his.

3
CHAPTER

George Randolph Pearkes, VC: Courage in Belgium

1917: Passchendaele

A bright moon shone over Belgium and France on the night of 29 October 1917. The First World War had ground on for more than three years. Clear in the moonlight, the opposing armies faced each other from their long lines of trenches, the Germans on one side, the Allied forces on the other. In between lay No Man's Land, a muddy wasteland of rubble and shell holes.

There was mud everywhere. It clung to boots, clothing, hands, hair. One of the muddiest parts of the whole front lay near the Belgian village of Passchendaele. The village itself, now in ruins, stood on a slight ridge.

Passchendaele, 1917. The constant shelling and heavy rains had turned the ground into a swamp

Below the ridge, countless exploding shells had turned the ground into a swamp.

This was the land over which George Randolph Pearkes had to lead his men into battle next morning. For several days, the Allies had tried to capture the ridge from the Germans, and many Canadians had already been killed. Tomorrow, they would make yet another assault. Even George Pearkes, who by nature looked on the bright side, knew that the next day was going to be grim.

After three years of war, George knew all about its horrors. He had seen friends killed, and he had twice been wounded. For weeks on end he had lived in an open trench, his clothes sodden from the rain, his feet permanently wet. He no longer felt the thrill he had felt when he first arrived in the front line and realized there was no one between himself and the enemy. Yet he still felt that same sense of loyalty and duty that had inspired William Hall at Lucknow.

In some ways, Pearkes and Hall were very similar. Both men stood rock-firm when the going got tough, providing strong support for their companions. Like Hall, Pearkes had purposely chosen a life of adventure when he was a teenager.

From England to Canada

Born at Watford, England, on 26 February 1888, and educated at private schools, George had set sail for Canada when he was 18 to train as a farmer so that he could homestead. He settled on a piece of land west of Stauffer, Alberta, and in 1909 spent his first winter there alone, shivering in a homemade shack.

His bed was a bundle of fir branches wrapped in blankets. His tables and chairs were boxes. His sink, a bucket of water that froze over each night. He had never known anything like this, and he loved it. But as the region gradually became more settled, homesteading lost its challenge. Soon George looked for adventure farther afield.

A year after this picture was taken, George set sail for Canada at age eighteen

George Pearkes

George Pearkes, (centre standing), and other members of the Dominion Lands Survey in 1912

For a while he worked as an axeman, chopping trees for a surveying team, travelling and camping in the bush north of Fort McMurray, Alberta. Then he joined the Royal North-West Mounted Police, serving on the Yukon-Alaska border. He was in the Mounties when the war started in 1914 and he had some difficulty getting released from the service so that he could volunteer for the army. But in March 1915, he enlisted with the Canadian Mounted Rifles.

He joined as a trooper but was soon promoted to corporal. He had reached the rank of major by the time he arrived at Passchendaele in 1917. He was commander of C Company, 5th Canadian Mounted Rifles.

Constable Pearkes, Royal North-West Mounted Police

"The Bravest Man I Ever Knew"

George was promoted so quickly because he was such a good leader. His men would have followed him anywhere. "He was the bravest man I ever knew," said one. As well as admiring him, the men trusted him. He always planned well, and he never asked others to do what he wouldn't do himself. The men also liked him. He cared about them and looked after their well-being. As an officer, he rode a horse. But on long route-marches he would march along with the men, giving up his horse to the men who seemed most tired.

Typically, he spent much of the night before Passchendaele visiting each of the men of C Company, making sure they all understood the plan of attack, chatting with them and trying to keep up their spirits. He also made sure that each man had a hot meal. They weren't likely to get another until the battle was over – if they survived at all. The Germans held Passchendaele ridge in force and could keep out of sight behind bushes and ruined buildings. By contrast, the Canadians had to attack from the open, advancing uphill across marshy ground. For much of the way, not even a tree gave protection.

Passchendaele

Among the many places where Canadian troops fought was Passchendaele, in Belgium. More than 15 000 soldiers were killed or wounded fighting for five square kilometres of ground.

Early next morning, 30 October, as night

gradually lightened to day, the Canadian attack began. First came a thundering barrage of gunfire. Then Pearkes led his company into the open, ready to move forward. At that moment, the German guns roared back, and George felt a terrible pain in his left thigh. He was thrown to the ground, half-dazed.

Onward, Though Wounded

As he lay on the ground, he realized that his men were looking down at him, wondering what to do next. "I've got to go on for a while," he thought, "wounded or not." So he struggled to his feet. Even though his left leg was stiff and painful, he moved forward, leading his men of C Company with him.

Their advance was especially slow because of the heavy, slippery mud, but they made progress. But as the day gradually dawned, Pearkes realized that only a few groups had struggled forward, rather than the massed attack that the Allies had planned. The German bombardment that had wounded him had also killed many men around him. The two companies that were supposed to advance with C Company had collapsed. This meant that the Germans could fire on Pearkes and his men from the flanks as well as the front.

The heavy mud at Passchendaele made the Canadians' advance slow and difficult

It took almost two weeks of determined fighting before the Canadian forces finally seized Passchendaele. During this one campaign alone, nine Canadians won the Victoria Cross.

So many of C Company were hit that only about 35 men remained when they reached their special target, a ruined farm. Nevertheless, led fearlessly by Pearkes, they seized the farm from the defending Germans. They also captured a second farm that had been the target of another company.

A Tough Spot

But they were in a tough spot. They had advanced farther than any other company and the Germans were determined to drive them back. Now 20 of them remained to hold the position. They took cover in shallow shell holes, firing at any Germans who tried to advance on them.

By this time, the wounded were making their way back to field hospitals for treatment. Several of them carried notes from Pearkes asking for reinforcements and more ammunition. But in broad daylight, few could reach him under German fire. During the afternoon, almost 100 men from another company tried to come to his aid. Only nine reached him.

Pearkes and his men had to hold out until dark. Time and again the Germans attacked his little group. Each time they failed to push the determined Canadians from their position.

Meanwhile, Pearkes crawled from shell hole to shell hole, giving his few remaining men words of encouragement. When darkness came and 200 reinforcements arrived to take over, Pearkes was the last to leave.

When he reached the Canadian lines late that night, his colonel could hardly believe the blood on Pearkes's uniform. Not once, in all the messages that he had sent back, had he mentioned that he was wounded.

World War I ended in November, 1918

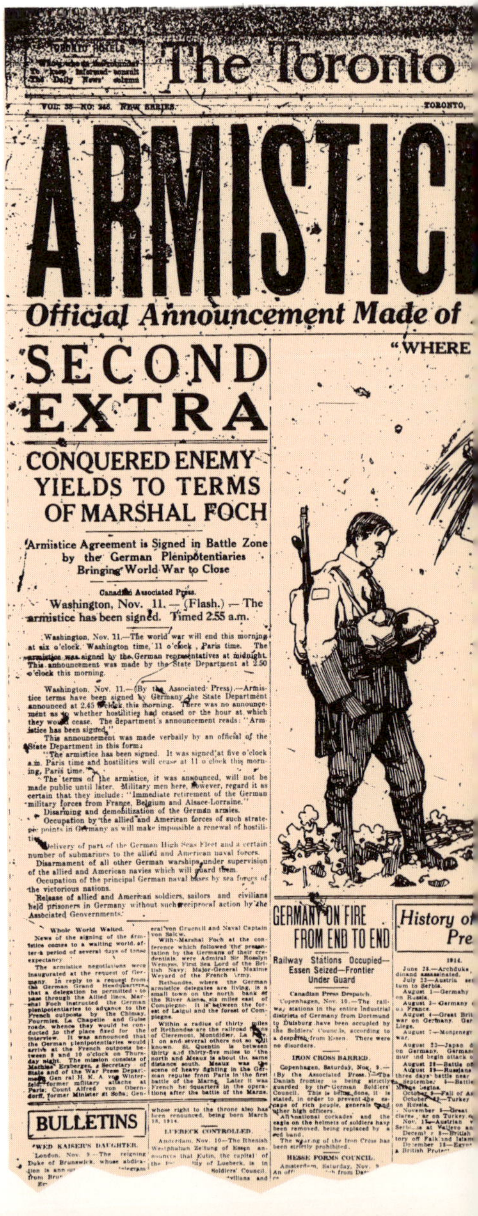

The Toronto

ARMISTICE

Official Announcement Made of

SECOND EXTRA

CONQUERED ENEMY YIELDS TO TERMS OF MARSHAL FOCH

Armistice Agreement is Signed in Battle Zone by the German Plenipotentiaries Bringing World War to Close

Canadian Associated Press.

Washington, Nov. 11.—(Flash.)—The armistice has been signed. Timed 2.55 a.m.

Washington, Nov. 11.—The world war will end this morning at six o'clock, Washington time, 11 o'clock, Paris time. The armistice was signed by the German representatives at midnight. This announcement was made by the State Department at 2.50 o'clock this morning.

Washington, Nov. 11.—(By the Associated Press).—Armistice terms have been signed by Germany the State Department announced at 2.45 o'clock this morning. There was no announcement as to whether hostilities had ceased or the hour at which they would cease. The department's announcement reads: "Armistice has been signed."

This announcement was made verbally by an official of the State Department in this form:

"The armistice has been signed. It was signed at five o'clock a.m. Paris time and hostilities will cease at 11 o'clock this morning, Paris time."

The terms of the armistice, it was announced, will not be made public until later. Military men here, however, regard it as certain that they include: "Immediate retirement of the German military forces from France, Belgium and Alsace-Lorraine."

Disarming and demobilization of the German armies.

Occupation by the allied and American forces of such strategic points in Germany as will make impossible a renewal of hostilities.

Delivery of part of the German High Seas Fleet and a certain number of submarines to the allied and American naval forces.

Disarmament of all other German warships under supervision of the allied and American navies which will guard them.

Occupation of the principal German naval bases by sea forces of the victorious nations.

Release of allied and American soldiers, sailors and civilians held prisoners in Germany without such reciprocal action by the Associated Geovernments.

Whole World Waited.

News of the signing of the armistice comes to a waiting world after a period of several days of tense expectancy.

GERMANY ON FIRE FROM END TO END

Railway Stations Occupied—Essen Seized—Frontier Under Guard

BULLETINS

The Victoria Cross

The colonel recommended Pearkes for the Victoria Cross. The official citation says that Pearkes showed "most conspicuous bravery" and "supreme contempt of danger and wonderful powers of control and leading."

By the time the war ended in November 1918, George had been wounded five times. As well, he had discovered what he had always suspected, that the army was the place for him. He stayed on after the war, reaching the rank of major-general.

In the Second World War, which began in 1939, he did not see active service, much to his disappointment. Instead, he was posted to British Columbia as the commander-in-chief, Pacific Command. At the time, there were great fears that Japan might invade British Columbia,

During his army career, George Pearkes had many outside interests. Early in the 1920s he organized and ran the 14th Troop of Boy Scouts of Calgary

Daily News

DOUBLE UP! Multiply your last Victory Loan subscription by two—and hurry up.

[NOV]EMBER 11, 1918. PRICE TWO CENTS.

IS SIGNED

[...]ement Bringing Hostilities to Close

[...]S GROW."

SOCIALIST HEADS NEW GOVERNMENT; REVOLT WIDENS

Berlin Garrison Quickly Goes Over and Little Bloodshed is Reported in Capital—Ebert's Becomes Chancellor

Canadian Press Despatch.

Berlin, Saturday, Nov. 9.—(German Wireless to London.)—Nov. 10. —(12.56 p.m.)—(By the Associated Press.)—The German People's Government has been instituted in the greater part of Berlin. The garrison has gone over to the Government. The Workmen's and Soldiers' Council has declared a general strike. Troops and machine guns have been placed at the disposal of the Council.

The Social-Democratic party is interceding (?) with the People's Government. The guards which had been stationed at the public offices and other buildings have been withdrawn.

Friedrich Ebert (Vice-president of the Social-Democrat party) is carrying on the Chancellorship.

BERLIN IS OCCUPIED.

Copenhagen, Nov. 10—(8.45 a.m.)—Berlin was occupied by forces of the Soldiers' and Workmen's Councils on Saturday afternoon according to a Wolff Bureau report received here.

MANY CITIES ARE SEIZED.

Copenhagen, Nov. 10.—Rebellions have occurred in Hanover, Cologne, Brunswick, and Magdeburg, according to the official announcement at Berlin. These cities, however, are not wholly in the hands of the mutineers, the statement adds. At Magdeburg the garrison resisted.

BLOODLESS REVOLUTION?

Basel, Nov. 10.—An official despatch received by the Havas Agency from Berlin to-day says:

"Official—The revolution has resulted in a striking victory almost without the effusion of blood.

"A general strike was declared this morning. It brought a cessation of work in all workshops at about [...] o'clock.

"A regiment of Nuremburg Chasseurs passed over to the people. Other troops rapidly followed their action.

"The Alexander Regiment, after hearing a declaration by Deputy Wells, went over to the revolution."

FIGHTING REPORTED.

London, Nov. 10.—8.57 a.m.—Severe fighting took place in Berlin between 6 and 8 o'clock last night, and a violent cannonade was heard from the heart of the city. The revolution is in full swing in Berlin and the Red Forces occupy the greater part of the German capital, according to a Copenhagen despatch to the Exchange Telegraph Company, quoting "Berlin advices sent from there at 3 o'clock this morning.

When revolutionaries attempted to enter a building in which they supposed a number of officers were concealed shots were fired from the windows. The Reds then began shelling the building.

Many persons were killed and wounded before the officers surrendered. The Red forces are in control and have restored order. [...] guards are marching through the streets.

The Crown Prince's palace has been seized by the revolutionists. The people are shouting "Long live the republic" and are singing the "Marseillaise."

When the cannonade began the people thought the Reichbank was being bombarded, and thousands rushed to the square in front of the Crown Prince's palace. It was later determined that other buildings were under fire.

CITIES FALL INTO LINE.

London, Nov. 10.—(11.2[...] a.m.)—Leipzig, the largest city in Saxony, Stuttgart, the capital of Wurttemberg, and Cologne and Frankfort have joined the revolution, according to reports from the Danish frontier telegraphed here by the Copenhagen correspondent of the Exchange Telegraph Company. Soldiers' councils at Stuttgart, [Co]logne and Frankfort have decided to proclaim a republic.

FORMER EMPEROR FLEES

William Hohezollnern Reported to be in Holland.

Canadian Press Despatch.

Washington, Nov. 10.—William Hohenzollern has arrived in Holland and is proceeding to the town of Desteeg, near Utrecht, according to a despatch received by the American general staff to-day from The Hague.

The message said:

"Press reports state that the Kaiser arrived this morning in Maastricht, Holland, and is proceeding to Middachten Castle, in the town of Desteeg, near Utrecht."

PEACEMAKER'S BIRTHDAY

Kaiser's Fall Comes on Notable Anniversary

It is a remarkable coincidence that the Kaiser, War Lord of Germany and apostle of violence, fell from power on November 9th, the birthday of King Edward VII., called the Peacemaker.

CROSS BELGIAN BORDER.

Paris, Nov. 9.—French cavalry has crossed the Belgian border, the War Office announces to-night. An advance of more than nine miles was made to-day at certain points.

EMPEROR SHIVERED AND THEN SIGNED

"It May be for the Good of Germany," Was Kaiser's Doubting Remark

Canadian Press Despatch.

London, Nov. 10.—(2.04 p.m.)—Emperor William signed a letter of abdication on Saturday morning at the German Grand Headquarters in the presence of Crown Prince Frederick William and Field Marshal Hindenburg, according to a despatch from Amsterdam to the Exchange Telegraph Company.

The German Crown Prince signed his renunciation to the throne shortly afterwards.

It is believed that King Ludwig of Bavaria and King Frederick August of Saxony also have abdicated.

The ex-Kaiser and the former Crown Prince were expected to take leave of their troops on Saturday, but nothing has been settled regarding their future movements.

Before placing his signature to the document an urgent [...] from Philipp Scheidemann, [...]

[...]ld War [in] Brief Form

[...]—President Wilson sends [a] protest to Germany.

[...]—Italy declares war on [...]

[...]—Austrians enter Lem[berg] [...]

EBERT, SOCIALIST, NAMED CHANCELLOR

Issues Proclamation Saying He Plans People's Government

Canadian Press Despatch.

Zurich, Nov. 10.—Because of the troubles in the interior of Germany, Prince Maximilian of Baden and all the Bourgeoisie Ministers have resigned, says a despatch from Berlin. Friedrich Ebert, the German Socialist leader, has been definitely recognized as Chancellor.

Copenhagen, Nov. 10—(8.30 a.m.)—Friedrich Ebert, the Socialist leader, has been appointed Imperial Chancellor. He has issued a proclamation saying that he plans to form a people's Government, which will endeavor to bring about speedy peace.

AT EBERT'S DISPOSAL.

[...]

and it was General Pearkes's job to defend the West Coast if there was an invasion.

The nearest he came to any action was to see some troops off to a remote Aleutian island which the Japanese had seized from the Americans. As the men boarded the ship, many received a boost from their commander-in-chief standing on the dock, shaking their hands and having photos taken so that he could send snaps to their families with their messages. Whether Pearkes was a corporal or a major-general, he never lost the knack of inspiring others, because he cared.

Minister of National Defence George Pearkes in Prime Minister John Diefenbaker's cabinet, 1957

Another Service

In 1945, he retired from the army after 30 years' service, only to serve his country in another role, as a Member of Parliament. He became a cabinet minister under John Diefenbaker in 1957, and was appointed Lieutenant-Governor of British Columbia in 1960. When he retired again in 1968, he was 80 years old. He died in Victoria in 1984 at the age of 96.

George Pearkes sometimes said that he was "lucky" to have been awarded the Victoria Cross. He didn't mean that it happened by accident; he meant that he was lucky to be one of the few recommended for the medal.

Only 93 Canadians ever received the VC. Sixty-nine of them won it during the First World War. Yet Pearkes felt that many more had earned the honour. "For every man who gets the VC, there are tens of thousands who are just as gallant," he said.

This was also true in the Second World War. In the first place, an act of heroism had to be seen and reported to qualify for a VC. Many brave deeds were never reported because nobody lived to tell the tale.

HIGHLIGHT OF RETIREMENT . . . a surprise party given by Saanich neighbors.

GENERAL PEARKES

— a man of energy and dedication

Se...
homesteadin...
ed for two and one ...
Mounted Police in the Yukon.

He enlisted in the Canadian Mounted ...
Victoria, B.C., in March of 1915. Seven months ...
with his unit in France.

He rose quickly through the ranks and was commissioned in the field in April, 1916.

He was promoted to Acting Captain in October of 1916 and to Acting Major two days later. He attained the rank of Acting Lieutenant-Colonel in January of 1918 and become a temporary Lieutenant-Colonel in March of the same year.

By the end of the First World War, Mr. Pearkes was commanding the 116th Battalion, Canadian Expeditionary Force.

He was wounded in action five times — twice seriously.

He was awarded the Victoria Cross while serving as a Major in 5 CMRs for gallantry at Passchendaele in 1917. He was earlier awarded the Military Cross for "conspicuous gallantry in action.

Mr. Pearkes was awarded the Distinguished Service Order for gallantry in action at Amiens. He was also awarded the French Croix de Guerre and was mentioned in Dispatches.

After the First World War, Mr. Pearkes remained in the Permanent Force as an Officer in Princess Patricia's Canadian

com...
this formation ...
to the rank of Major Ge...
First Division.

In September, 1942, Mr. Pearkes was ap...
Officer Commanding, Pacific Command, and remaine...
appointment until February of 1945.

During the Second World War he was created a Companion of the Order of the Bath. He was also awarded the United States Order of Merit.

Mr. Pearkes entered the political field as a Member of Parliament for Nanaimo, B.C., in June of 1945. In the House of Commons, Mr. Pearkes interested himself principally in Defence, External Affairs, Veterans' Affairs and Fisheries.

He was appointed Minister of National Defence in the Progressive Conservative Cabinet on June 21, 1957 — a post he held until October of 1960 when he became Lieutenant-Governor of British Columbia.

The First World War

The First World War began in 1914. It involved disputes over land and power. On one side were forces from Austria-Hungary, Germany, Bulgaria, and Turkey. On the other side were the allies, an alliance of 12 countries. Chief among them were France, Great Britain, Russia, and the United States.

As part of the British Empire, Canada entered the war in August, when Britain declared war on Germany. A total of 424 589 Canadian soldiers fought in Belgium and France. Of these, 60 661 were killed. Another 9600 officers and men fought in the Canadian naval services, of whom 150 lost their lives. Canada had no air force of her own, but 22 000 Canadians joined the British flying services. More than one-quarter of all pilots in these services were Canadian. Of Canadian fliers, 1563 were killed.

The First World War ended on November 11, 1918, after the German alliance surrendered. By then, more than 10 million soldiers from all the countries involved had lost their lives.

A Canadian batallion going "over the top" (leaving the trenches for an attack across No Man's Land), 1916

Canada's most famous hero from the First World War was William Avery "Billy" Bishop, the intrepid fighter pilot. Bishop won the VC for making a solo attack on a German airfield that was more than 25 kilometres inside German-held territory. Most of the VC winners in the First World War were soldiers. Like George Pearkes, they endured the misery of life in the trenches as well as rising to great heights of courage.

4
CHAPTER

Andrew Mynarski, VC: Courage in Flight

No One Special

Andrew Mynarski never knew he had won the Victoria Cross. The medal was conferred on him after he was dead. Had he known about it, he would probably have been surprised as well as pleased. He would have been even more surprised to learn that he was one of Canada's national heroes, with fly-pasts held in his honour, and a school in Winnipeg and a group of Manitoba lakes named after him, as well as a Winnipeg branch of the Royal Canadian Legion.

As a child in Winnipeg, Andrew never thought of himself as anything special. Slim and

Andrew Mynarski

dark haired, he was rather quiet until you got to know him. Then he was good fun, as his friends all agreed. But he was one of the gang, not a leader, and though he loved playing hockey and baseball, he was not good enough at either sport to make the school team.

In fact, Andrew was like most of the other kids at King Edward School in Winnipeg – good at some things, not so good at others. Nor did he want to be any different. He certainly didn't dream of a life of adventure far from home. His main ambition was to get a steady job so that he could marry and live comfortably. He hoped to be able to buy some of the things he had done without as a child: a radio, a camera, a record player. His family could not afford such luxuries.

King Edward School in Winnipeg, Manitoba, where Andrew went to school

Andrew's parents couldn't even afford to buy toys for their children. Andrew's few toys were homemade. His parents had come from Poland five years before he was born, and they were still struggling to settle into their new country. Although his father had found work with the railways, it didn't bring in much money, and most of that went towards the rent on their home.

A Winnipeg Childhood

The Mynarskis lived in the north end of Winnipeg, at 846 Manitoba Avenue, where Andrew was born on 14 October 1916. He was the second oldest of six children, three boys and three girls.

As the second oldest in the family, Andrew pitched in to help as much as he could. Each evening, after he had done his homework, he and his older brother, Chester, chopped firewood for the stove. They had to do this chore in summer as well as winter, because their mother cooked on a wood-burning stove. Sometimes, Andrew helped out in the yard, digging potatoes or beets. The Mynarskis lived almost entirely on what they could grow, and they'd turned their whole yard into a vegetable garden.

Members of the Polish community in Andrew's neighbourhood watch the Corpus Christi parade near the church

St. John Cantius Church was close to Andrew's home

Most families in the neighbourhood were in a similar position. Many had also come from Poland. Like them, Andrew grew up under Polish and Canadian influences.

One day he would meet his friends at the Exhibition Grounds to play hockey at the rink; next day he would meet them with their parents at Sokol, the Polish cultural centre. Andrew could speak and read Polish, and he once acted in a play at Sokol.

Another common meeting place was St. John Cantius Church, a few blocks from the Mynarski home. Religion played a large role in Andrew's home life, especially at times like Christmas, when his family continued many traditions. But at Christmas in 1932 there were no cheerful celebrations in the Mynarski home. That year the tree was draped in black, in mourning for Andrew's father, who had just died of tuberculosis.

For Mrs. Mynarski, her husband's death brought a crisis as well as a tragedy. Canada was in the midst of the Depression. Millions of people had no jobs. Thousands of companies had closed down. How was she to provide for her children without her husband's pay? Although Andrew's older brother, Chester, found work whenever he could get it, he didn't bring in nearly enough to support the family. Andrew was 16 at the time and had just moved

During the Depression, millions of Canadians were out of work. Some joined demonstrations and marches in protest

to Isaac Newton School for Grade 10. But he realized he couldn't stay there. He would have to go to work. In fact, he had already been earning some money by cutting leather in the evenings for a Winnipeg furrier. Now he left school so that he could work for the furrier full-time.

Second World War

The Second World War began in September, 1939, after Germany invaded Poland. On one side were the axis powers: Germany, Italy, Japan, and Hungary, Bulgaria, and Romania. Opposing them were the allies: Canada, Britain, France, the Soviet Union, the United States, Australia, Belgium, Brazil, China, Denmark, Greece, Netherlands, New Zealand, Poland, Norway, South Africa, and Yugoslavia.

More than a million Canadians participated in the war, including almost 50 000 women. The war lasted six years and was fought throughout the world, though the areas most affected were Europe and the Pacific.

Germany surrendered in May, 1945. In August, the first atomic bomb was dropped by U.S. forces on Hiroshima. Japan surrendered in early September.

Andrew had already discovered his talent for making things with his hands. He made carefully crafted metal ashtrays, model airplanes, lockets for his sisters, and beautifully finished pieces of furniture, which the family still own. In the back shed of the Mynarski home on Manitoba Avenue, he built himself a small woodworking shop. Until he joined the Royal Canadian Air Force during the Second World War, he spent most of his spare time there.

The Second World War Begins

When the Second World War began in 1939, Andrew did not feel that it concerned him much, in spite of Germany's invasion of Poland. His main concern was to provide his mother with the support she needed to feed and clothe her younger children. But as the German tanks rolled across Europe, overrunning one country after another, Andrew became far more aware of the situation. By the summer of 1940, Germany had captured most of Europe and was threatening to invade England.

By this time, Chester had left home to join the army. So Andrew signed on with the army reserve. This meant that he could keep his job while doing his soldiering on weekends. But as time passed, this didn't seem enough. Some of his friends had volunteered for the Royal Canadian Air Force, and in September 1941, Andrew did too. He signed on at the recruiting centre in Winnipeg and then went home and told his mother. One week later he started his training at the RCAF depot in Edmonton.

After more than a year, Andrew became a fully qualified air gunner with the rank of sergeant. Then he said goodbye to his family and his fiancée, Victoria, and took the train to Halifax. There he boarded a troop ship for England. In January 1943, at the age of 26, Andrew Charles Mynarski took his last look at the land of his birth and went off to war.

The Winnipeg newspapers were filled with news of the outbreak of World War II

4th Extra The Winnipeg Tribune — THE PRICE OF THIS EXTRA IS FIVE Cents

50th Year — WINNIPEG, FRIDAY, SEPTEMBER 1, 1939 — No. 209

CEASE FIRE OR WE FIGHT BRITAIN TELLS GERMANY

Withdraw Or It's War, Is Chamberlain Warning

LONDON, Sept. 1—(Passed by British censor)—Prime Minister Chamberlain declared tonight that unless Germany would suspend aggressive action and withdraw her forces from Poland Great Britain would unhesitatingly fulfil her obligations to Poland.

Mr. Chamberlain began his address to the House of Commons at 6.08 p.m. (11.08 a.m. C.S.T.).

He was greeted with a roar of cheers, and waved solemnly in acknowledgment.

There were cries of "God bless you!" and "Good luck!"

"I do not propose to say many words tonight; the time has come when action rather than speech is required," Mr. [illegible]

Fight And Conquer!

The Situation At A Glance

German troops and aircraft have invaded Poland.

Poland has called for aid from Great Britain and France.

Great Britain and France have ordered general mobilization.

The British parliament has been called to meet at 11 a.m., C.S.T.

CANADA PUT ON WAR BASIS

OTTAWA, Sept. 1—The War Measures Act of 1914, giving the government extraordinary powers to act in emergency pending the assembly of Parliament, was proclaimed by order-in-council adopted at a meeting of the government early today.

The War Measures Act, which came into being in 1914, gives the government wide measures of control over shipping, censorship, trade and commerce, expropriation of private property, transportation and other matters relating to the security of the realm.

OTTAWA, Sept. 1.—Prime Minister Mackenzie King announced at one o'clock today that the military, naval and air force have been placed on an [illegible] service footing.

The Lancaster bomber

Flight into Danger

Like many other Canadians, Andrew was stationed in England. From there he went on bombing raids over German-held Europe. He flew mainly in Lancasters, and during the next year, he became used to crouching in the bomber's gun turret as he searched the night sky for enemy fighters. The bombers would set out at dusk and often not return till dawn, if they returned at all.

On the night of 12 June 1944, Mynarski and the rest of 419 Squadron were bound for the railway yards at Cambrai in France. He was the mid-upper gunner on a seven-man crew. His closest friend on the crew was Pat Brophy, the rear gunner.

As usual, while waiting for take-off, Brophy and Mynarski sat on the grass beside the Lancaster, joking together as they tried to control their fear. Then Mynarski found a four-leafed clover in the grass. Twirling it cheerfully, he gave it to Brophy. "A sign of good luck," he said. A quarter of an hour later, the Lancaster was roaring through the sky, heading for France, with the gunners isolated in their turrets. Their only connection was the intercom.

"Estimating 80 minutes to target," came the voice of their pilot, Art deBreyne.

"Thanks," said Andrew. "No rush."

They were scarcely over the French coast when they were caught in the beam of a searchlight. From the ground, the anti-aircraft guns began to fire at them. Art deBreyne threw the plane into a dive, twisting and banking to escape the dazzling light. A few minutes later, they were safely in the dark again.

They didn't realize that a German fighter had staked them out and was now following at a distance. Suddenly Brophy saw the fighter attacking from underneath their plane. Yelling a warning, he swung his gun turret around and opened fire. Already the fighter was tearing past, guns blazing. Three enormous explosions rocked the Lancaster, destroying both its port engines and setting it on fire.

April 1944 – Andrew poses with the rest of the crew in front of one of the airplanes he flew in

Bail Out!

As deBreyne fought to keep the plane steady, he flashed the signal for the crew to bail out. Four of the crew had jumped from the forward hatch before he fastened his parachute and prepared to follow. He couldn't see the rear hatch, but he was sure he was the last to leave: Mynarski and Brophy had had plenty of time to bail out.

In fact, they were still on the plane. Mynarski had been standing at the rear hatch, just about to jump, when he caught sight of Brophy and realized that his friend was trapped inside his gun turret. Brophy was struggling frantically with the rotating gear. When he had swung the turret around to fire on the German plane, it had stuck in that position, and now he couldn't open the turret's doors.

Mynarski turned away from the hatch and began to move up the plane. "Don't try it!" shouted Brophy, waving him back, for the fuselage between them was on fire, fuelled by spilled oil. Besides, the plane was going to crash in a few minutes. Already it was lurching so violently that Mynarski couldn't walk upright. He got down on his hands and knees, and then crawled towards Brophy through the flaming oil.

Mynarski's pants and gloves caught fire long before he reached Brophy. And then he couldn't open the gun turret. He pulled at it furiously, then tried to batter it open with a fire axe. Nothing worked.

"Go back!" shouted Brophy. "Save yourself!"

Reluctantly, Mynarski crawled back towards the hatch. Then, though his parachute and flying suit were a blaze of fire, he paused to offer his friend a final gesture of encouragement. Drawing himself up smartly, he saluted. Then he turned and jumped.

Some members of the French Resistance, who were watching from the ground, said that Mynarski looked like a ball of flame hurtling from the plane. They went to his aid as soon as he landed, but he was too badly burnt. He died that night.

One Witness Survives

No one would have known this story if Brophy had not survived. At the last moment, the plane hit a tree, and the impact broke open the rear turret, hurling Brophy free. So he was not in the Lancaster when it hit the ground seconds later. Nor was Brophy badly hurt. Although he was knocked out, he did not break a single bone. He walked away from the crash and took shelter in a French farm. There he was met by members of the Resistance. They kept him hidden from the Germans until they could see him on his way to England.

The other crew members also survived, and most were safely hidden by the Resistance. The German army caught only two and sent them to prison camp. Meanwhile, the RCAF thought that Mynarski, too, was a prisoner. He had been due for promotion to pilot officer, and his promotion was quickly approved, because officers were given privileged treatment in prison camp. Three months passed before Brophy at last reached England and told his story to RCAF officials.

If Brophy had died in the crash or if he had been killed before he reached England, no

Pat Brophy was Andrew's closest friend in the crew. Brophy went down in the crash but survived

"He was a mass of flames below the waist," said Pat Brophy. "Seeing him like that, I forgot everthing else. 'Go back, Andy! Get out!' I shouted."

Pat Brophy stayed on in the RCAF and now lives at St. Catharines, Ontario.

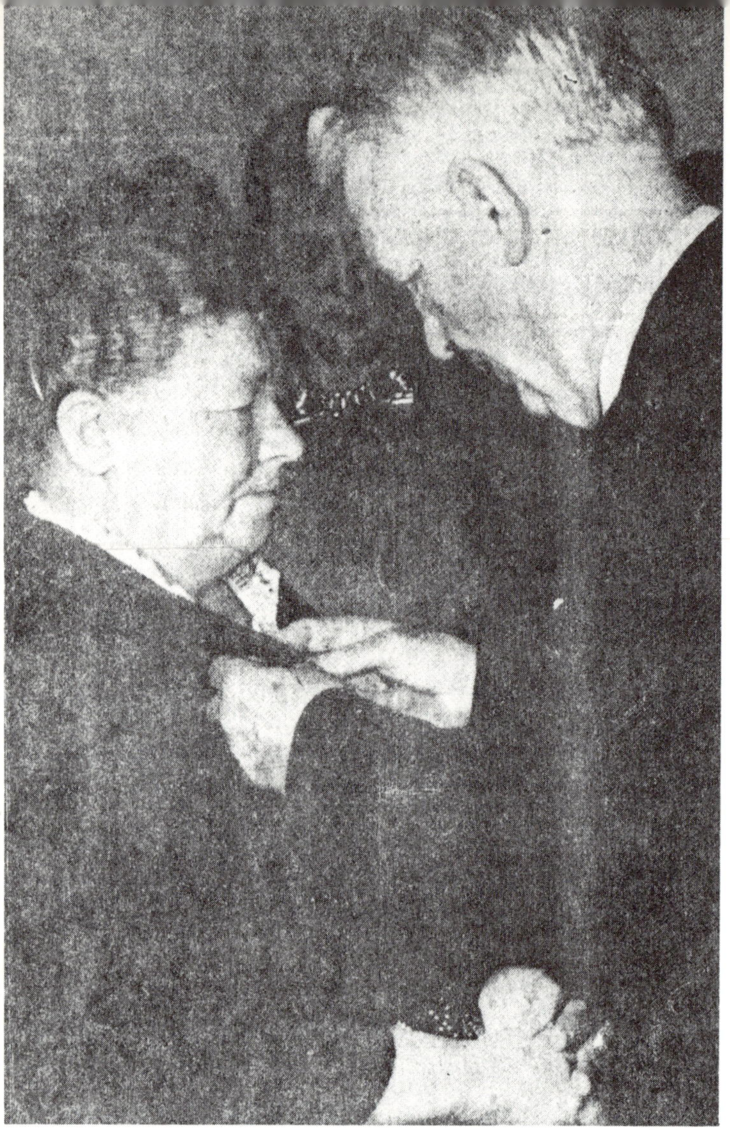

The Lieutenant-Governor of Manitoba presents Andrew's mother with Andrew's Victoria Cross

one would have known about Mynarski's act of heroism. Like thousands of other victims of war, Andrew Mynarski would have been listed simply as "killed in action." His mother would not have had the consolation of accepting the Victoria Cross on his behalf from the Lieutenant-Governor of Manitoba. And generations of Canadians would not have gained inspiration from this Winnipeg boy who never thought he would do anything special with his life.

CHAPTER 5

The Nature of Bravery

More Than Physical

When reading about very brave people, it is easy to think, "I could never be like them. They're different."

But are they so very different?

None of us knows how we will act when faced with an emergency. Even if at some time we have let our friends down by panicking or by running away, we can act differently another time. Often the private knowledge of past failure helps people to do better and act with great courage.

Since 1972, 14 Canadians have won the Cross of Valour, and more than a thousand have won the Star of Courage and the Medal of Bravery. Yet even they are only a very small percentage of the people who show outstanding courage. In every hospital in the country, for example, brave children fight their own private battles against pain and death. The public seldom hears of them.

Other people show bravery in different ways. In fact, bravery involves more than physical courage. It can require moral courage, as well. People who do the right thing, even at the risk of being laughed at or ridiculed, show bravery. But their bravery is not always recognized.

Some people think that it is a mistake to give medals, because so many worthy people never receive them. Yet medals show that we value courage. They are a way of saying thank-you, and of remembering and honouring a few of the very bravest among us.

Many young people have won bravery awards:

CROSS OF VALOUR

Thomas Hynes, aged 19

Thomas Hynes dived into a frozen pond and saved his 8-year-old cousin, who had fallen in. Because of the effort involved and the bitter cold, Thomas himself did not survive.

STAR OF COURAGE

Reginald Wettlaufer, aged 14

Reginald risked his life and almost drowned while attempting to save a friend who was caught in the current of a spillway.

The Star of Courage is awarded for acts of conspicuous courage in circumstances of great peril

MEDAL OF BRAVERY
James Piecowye, aged 9

James towed three boys and his grandfather to shore after their boat overturned at Fishing Lake, Saskatchewan. As his grandfather weakened, James held his head above water and then tried to apply artificial respiration. Despite his efforts, his grandfather died, but the others reached shore safely.

MEDAL OF BRAVERY
Robert Forbes, aged 11

Robert Forbes entered a burning tent and rescued his sister, who was trapped inside it.

MEDAL OF BRAVERY
Gyuala Lakatar, Johnson Gock and Rupert Fong

The three boys rushed to the aid of the vice-principal of their school in Kelowna, whose clothes caught fire when he was refilling his gas tank and static electricity ignited the gasoline. Their prompt and courageous action saved his life.

The Medal of Bravery is awarded for acts of bravery in hazardous circumstances

1

2